The Story of Imam Muslim

MAA

Published by MAA, 2025.

THE STORY OF IMAM MUSLIM

First edition. September 9, 2025.

ISBN: 979-8232243296

Written by MAA.

Chapter 1: The World of Imam Muslim's Birth

In the early decades of the third century after the Hijrah, the city of Naysabur in the region of Khurasan was alive with movement, thought, and a deep hunger for knowledge. This was the world into which **Muslim ibn al-Hajjaj** would be born in the year 206 AH (821 CE). His birthplace was not an ordinary settlement but one of the intellectual capitals of the Islamic world. Naysabur had grown into a center where merchants, theologians, poets, and jurists crossed paths, each contributing to the vibrancy of its culture.

The Abbasid Caliphate was at its height during this period, commanding authority from Baghdad over a vast and diverse empire. The empire stretched from the borders of North Africa to the lands of Central Asia, uniting peoples of different languages, traditions, and philosophies. Within this broad political framework, Khurasan played a special role. It was a frontier province, strategically important and culturally rich, a place where the traditions of Persia merged with the growing influence of Islam. The city of Naysabur, in particular, stood as a beacon of scholarship, trade, and religious activity.

Life in Naysabur was shaped by its unique geographical position. Situated along the Silk Road, it became a meeting point for travellers, scholars, and traders from faraway regions such as India, Transoxiana, and the Arabian Peninsula. The exchange of goods—silks, spices, manuscripts—was accompanied by the exchange of ideas. Philosophy, medicine, and mathematics were being debated alongside theology and law, and the thirst for learning defined the city's atmosphere.

The intellectual climate of the early third century AH was also deeply shaped by debates surrounding the interpretation of Islam itself. Questions about theology, the attributes of God, and the authority of hadith occupied the minds of scholars and ordinary Muslims alike. In

Baghdad, the heart of the Caliphate, the rationalist movement known as the Mu'tazilah had found support in certain periods, influencing theological discussions across the empire. Yet in places like Khurasan, there was a strong defense of traditionalism, where scholars emphasized reliance on the Qur'an and the authentic sayings of the Prophet Muhammad. This climate of debate and differing perspectives created both tension and progress in the world of Islamic thought.

The importance of hadith in this period cannot be overstated. By the time of Imam Muslim's birth, a century and a half had already passed since the Prophet's death, and the need to carefully preserve his words and actions had become urgent. While many scholars dedicated their lives to this task, challenges had also arisen. Fabricated narrations circulated, often introduced for political or sectarian motives, and distinguishing the true from the false required rigorous scholarship. This was the scholarly mission of the age: to safeguard the Sunnah of the Prophet with accuracy and discipline.

Naysabur provided fertile ground for this mission. The city's mosques were not merely places of prayer but centers of learning, where circles of students gathered around teachers, memorizing, questioning, and debating. Libraries began to take form, and scholars from across the Islamic world visited the city to exchange knowledge. The people of Khurasan were known for their respect for learning and their willingness to support scholars materially and socially, ensuring that the pursuit of knowledge remained a noble calling.

At the same time, the world into which Imam Muslim was born was not free of hardship. The Abbasid Empire, though strong, faced internal unrest. Political rivalries, tribal disputes, and occasional uprisings threatened stability. For scholars, this meant that their work required not only dedication but also wisdom to navigate the complexities of authority and politics. The transmission of knowledge was never separate from the realities of power, and scholars often had to balance their devotion to truth with the pressures of their environment.

Into this rich yet challenging world, Imam Muslim opened his eyes. He was born into a society where the preservation of faith and knowledge was seen as a sacred duty, where scholars carried immense responsibility, and where the intellectual currents of the time demanded clarity, precision, and integrity.

Chapter 2: Early Life in Naysabur

Muslim ibn al-Hajjaj was born in the year 206 AH (821 CE) in the thriving city of Naysabur, a place that would leave a lasting mark on his character and intellectual journey. His family belonged to the Persian population of Khurasan, a region long celebrated for producing scholars, poets, and leaders of thought. The details of his immediate household are scarce, but it is clear that he was raised in an environment where faith, discipline, and respect for knowledge were considered essential virtues.

From a young age, Muslim grew up surrounded by the religious culture of Naysabur. The call to prayer echoed across the city's neighbourhoods, mosques were filled with gatherings of students and teachers, and public life was intertwined with faith. In such a setting, the education of children often began early. Boys were taught the Qur'an as a foundation, not only for memorization but also as a moral compass guiding their future. Muslim followed this path, learning to recite and understand the words of God in his formative years. This early connection to the Qur'an laid the groundwork for the seriousness with which he would later approach the sayings of the Prophet.

Naysabur's vibrant intellectual environment also meant that children with aptitude were often introduced to broader studies at a young age. In addition to Qur'an recitation, students learned Arabic grammar, which was indispensable for anyone who aspired to scholarship. Though Persian was the common tongue in Khurasan, mastery of Arabic was essential, for it was the language of revelation and the medium of scholarship across the Islamic world. Muslim showed a natural attentiveness to language, and his early lessons in grammar and literature provided him with tools that would prove crucial in analyzing and authenticating narrations.

The atmosphere of Naysabur encouraged ambition. The city was known for its bustling marketplaces and caravans arriving from distant lands, but just as important was its status as a gathering point for scholars. Young Muslim would have seen respected teachers surrounded by groups of students, their discussions often extending deep into the day. For a child growing up in this environment, the image of a scholar was one of both prestige and devotion. Such impressions likely stirred in him the desire to dedicate his life to study.

As he grew older, Muslim began attending lessons in the mosques of Naysabur, where he was introduced to the study of hadith. These early sessions exposed him to the painstaking methods used by teachers to trace chains of narration and assess the reliability of transmitters. While at first this was merely an introduction, it awakened in him a fascination with the precision and care required in this field. By adolescence, he had already begun collecting narrations, a sign of his serious inclination toward hadith that distinguished him from his peers.

The influence of family cannot be overlooked in these years. Though little is recorded about his parents, the fact that he was able to devote himself so fully to scholarship suggests that his family provided him with both support and encouragement. In Khurasan, families who valued knowledge often considered the pursuit of learning to be a form of service to God and community, and they took pride in guiding their children toward scholarship. Muslim's upbringing was thus not only religious in practice but also intellectually nurturing, offering him both stability and inspiration.

By the time he reached his teenage years, Muslim had already acquired a reputation as a promising student in Naysabur. His teachers noticed his sharp memory, his seriousness in study, and his ability to distinguish details that others might overlook. Unlike many young men who divided their attention between trade, family responsibilities, or leisure, Muslim directed his focus almost entirely toward learning. The seeds of his future greatness were already visible, even if only in quiet form, in the way he approached his early education with discipline and sincerity.

Chapter 3: First Steps into Knowledge

As Muslim ibn al-Hajjaj grew into his teenage years, the foundation laid in his early education began to take shape in a more purposeful direction. What had started as the memorization of the Qur'an and the basics of language gradually transitioned into the disciplined study of hadith. In the Naysabur of his youth, scholarly gatherings were frequent, and young seekers of knowledge could find circles dedicated to Qur'anic exegesis, law, theology, and narration. For Muslim, it was the science of hadith that drew his heart and mind with unusual intensity.

The city's mosques and teaching circles offered him his first opportunities to engage with recognized scholars. Among his earliest teachers in Naysabur were local traditionists who emphasized the importance of strict authentication. They trained their students not merely to memorize narrations but to examine the integrity of their transmitters and to understand the nuances of the chains of transmission. Under their guidance, Muslim began to develop habits that would define his scholarship: attentiveness to detail, patience in listening, and caution in repeating what he had not verified.

His introduction to hadith was not limited to listening and memorizing. As was common in those days, students were encouraged to keep notebooks, carefully recording what they heard from their teachers. These early compilations served as both study aids and personal records of transmission. Muslim's notebooks would later be recognized for their order and accuracy, traits that reflected his methodical personality even in his youth. This discipline distinguished him from many of his contemporaries and built the reputation of a student who treated knowledge with seriousness and responsibility.

The first narrations he learned were often passed down within his city, where chains of transmission linked Naysabur's scholars back to earlier authorities in Iraq, the Hijaz, and beyond. Through these sessions, Muslim gained awareness of the wider scholarly world. He began to hear names of renowned traditionists in Baghdad, Basra, and Kufa, and stories of their travels and struggles in the pursuit of knowledge. These accounts stirred his imagination and planted the idea that his own education could not remain confined to Naysabur alone.

The atmosphere of learning was not without its challenges. The third century AH was a time when fabricated hadith had become a serious problem. Political disputes, sectarian rivalries, and personal agendas had led some individuals to invent sayings and attribute them falsely to the Prophet. Teachers in Naysabur repeatedly warned their students of this danger, urging them to exercise caution and to learn only from reliable authorities. For a young Muslim, these warnings were deeply instructive. They sharpened his awareness of the sacred duty carried by hadith scholars and instilled in him a determination to guard the Sunnah with integrity.

Alongside his formal learning, Muslim also absorbed the etiquette of studentship. Respect for teachers, humility in questioning, and patience in study were as important as the knowledge itself. In Naysabur, it was common for students to spend long hours in the company of their teachers, observing not only their words but also their character. Muslim learned that true scholarship was not measured by memorization alone but by piety, reliability, and moral conduct. This understanding left a lasting impression on him, shaping both his learning and his personal life.

By the end of his formative years in Naysabur, Muslim had moved beyond the stage of a casual learner. He had memorized hundreds of narrations, developed the ability to assess chains of transmission, and earned the trust of his teachers as a diligent and honest student. More importantly, he had gained clarity about his path. While many of his peers would eventually turn to law, commerce, or family responsibilities, Muslim's direction was firmly set. His first steps into knowledge had given him not only skill but also purpose, preparing him for the journeys of study that awaited him beyond his hometown.

Chapter 4: The Culture of Scholarship

In the third century after the Hijrah, scholarship in the Islamic world was not a pursuit reserved for a select few; it was the heartbeat of society. Cities like Baghdad, Basra, Kufa, Merv, and Naysabur thrived as centers of learning, attracting students and teachers from across the vast territories of the Abbasid Caliphate. For young Muslim ibn al-Hajjaj, this culture of knowledge provided the backdrop against which his own studies unfolded, shaping both his ambitions and his method.

The Abbasid era is often described as the golden age of Islamic civilization, and for good reason. Political authority, though sometimes turbulent, provided enough stability for scholarship to flourish. Wealth from trade routes and agricultural production supported institutions of learning and allowed communities to invest in libraries, mosques, and schools. Knowledge was not viewed as a luxury but as a duty, and scholars were held in high regard for their service to religion and society.

At the center of this scholarly culture stood the mosque. More than a place of worship, the mosque was the hub of intellectual life. Circles of students gathered around teachers to hear lessons in Qur'anic commentary, jurisprudence, theology, and above all, hadith. These gatherings were open to anyone with the patience to listen and the discipline to learn. A young seeker could find himself sitting shoulder to shoulder with merchants, craftsmen, and even officials, all united by their pursuit of understanding. For Muslim, this environment made scholarship accessible while also reminding him that knowledge was meant to serve the community.

Travel was another defining feature of the scholarly world. Unlike in later centuries, knowledge was not centralized in books alone but lived in the memories of transmitters. A student who wished to gain authentic narrations had to journey to the regions where reliable authorities lived. This practice, known as *rihla fi talab al-'ilm*—the journey in search of knowledge—was considered both a scholarly necessity and an act of devotion. Accounts of scholars traveling across deserts, boarding ships, and enduring hardship for the sake of a single narration were common, and these stories inspired new generations of students, including Muslim.

The methods of scholarship were marked by rigor. The sciences of hadith developed precise criteria for evaluating narrations, including the reliability of transmitters, the continuity of the chain, and the consistency of the text. To preserve accuracy, scholars memorized thousands of narrations and kept meticulous notes, often comparing what they had learned with fellow students. Debate and questioning were encouraged, but always within the framework of respect for teachers and adherence to evidence. This culture of scrutiny cultivated minds trained to differentiate between authentic and weak material, a skill that would become central to Muslim's life's work.

Beyond the religious sciences, the intellectual atmosphere of the time was enriched by encounters with philosophy, medicine, mathematics, and literature. While Muslim himself remained devoted to hadith, he grew up in a world where libraries stored translations of Greek texts, where debates on logic and theology were commonplace, and where poetry was celebrated as an art form. The presence of such diversity deepened the respect given to knowledge in all its forms, reinforcing the idea that learning elevated both individuals and societies.

Respect for scholars extended beyond the classroom. Communities often supported their teachers through gifts, stipends, or employment that allowed them the freedom to study and teach. Scholars, in turn, carried immense moral responsibility. They were expected to embody honesty, humility, and fairness, for their reputations determined the credibility of their transmission. For a young student like Muslim, this meant that scholarship was not simply about collecting information but about adopting a way of life rooted in integrity.

The culture of scholarship in which Imam Muslim was raised was therefore one of discipline, dedication, and reverence. It offered him role models who sacrificed comfort for knowledge, communities that cherished the preservation of faith, and institutions that sustained the pursuit of truth. Within this environment, his own journey from a promising student to a leading traditionist found both inspiration and structure.

Chapter 5: Nurturing a Passion for Hadith

By the time Muslim ibn al-Hajjaj reached the years of early maturity, the science of hadith had already established itself as the defining pursuit of his life. While many students divided their attention between various disciplines, he found himself drawn increasingly toward the sayings of the Prophet. What began as curiosity in the teaching circles of Naysabur soon grew into a serious commitment, one that demanded time, sacrifice, and discipline.

Hadith study in his era required more than memorization. It demanded a lifelong devotion to careful listening, precise recording, and constant verification. Young Muslim's teachers instilled in him the principle that not every report attributed to the Prophet could be trusted without scrutiny. This awareness deepened his fascination with the field. He came to see the science of hadith as both a religious obligation and a noble calling: to separate the authentic words of the Messenger from those that were fabricated or flawed. The responsibility carried immense weight, and Muslim approached it with the seriousness of one who recognized its sacred nature.

His early lessons involved learning chains of transmission, known as isnad. He quickly grasped the importance of tracing a narration back through reliable transmitters, evaluating the character, memory, and accuracy of each link in the chain. While other students might have been content with the outward text of a report, Muslim immersed himself in understanding the methods by which authenticity was judged. This focus distinguished him from his peers and demonstrated a maturity beyond his years.

Passion for hadith also meant long hours spent in gatherings where narrations were recited and compared. Students like Muslim would sit attentively, noting small differences in wording, and later return to their notes for review. Such dedication required both sharp memory and patience, qualities he seemed to possess in abundance. Teachers recognized in him a reliability that was rare among students, and they began to entrust him with greater responsibility, encouraging him to engage with narrations more critically.

The broader atmosphere of the time added urgency to his pursuit. Fabricated reports continued to circulate widely, introduced into sermons, legal debates, and even political disputes. The danger of misrepresenting the Prophet was a matter that deeply troubled sincere scholars. For Muslim, this reality turned his academic interest into a spiritual mission. He began to see hadith preservation as a form of service to the ummah, a defense of the Prophet's legacy against distortion.

As he advanced, Muslim started to collect narrations directly from visiting scholars who passed through Naysabur. Travellers from Iraq, the Hijaz, and beyond often brought with them chains of transmission not yet known in Khurasan. Muslim took every opportunity to sit in their company, record their narrations, and expand his knowledge. These encounters opened a window into the wider scholarly world and planted in him the desire to travel farther in search of authentic reports.

His passion also shaped his character. The discipline of hadith demanded humility, for even the most learned scholar had to submit to the evidence of transmission. Muslim absorbed this lesson early. He approached teachers with respect, refrained from rushing to opinions without verification, and treated each narration as a trust. This humility, combined with his growing mastery, earned him admiration among his fellow students.

By the close of his youth in Naysabur, Muslim's commitment to hadith had set him apart. He was no longer merely a promising student of general sciences but a young traditionist whose life was becoming defined by one pursuit: to seek, preserve, and authenticate the sayings of the Prophet with precision and devotion.

Chapter 6: Setting Out on Travels

In the world of third-century Islam, the path of true scholarship required more than attending local gatherings. The transmission of knowledge lived in the hearts and memories of men and women spread across the lands of the Abbasid Caliphate. To collect hadith and verify their chains, students had to leave their homes, endure long journeys, and sit before scholars in distant cities. This tradition of *rihla fi talab al-'ilm*—the journey in search of knowledge—was both a scholarly necessity and a form of devotion. For Muslim ibn al-Hajjaj, it became the defining stage of his growth.

Having already distinguished himself in Naysabur, Muslim recognized that remaining in his hometown could only take him so far. The teachers he had learned from encouraged their students to travel, for the science of hadith demanded breadth as well as depth. Each city held its own networks of transmitters, and only by seeking them out could a student hope to assemble a reliable and extensive collection. With this in mind, Muslim prepared to set out on the road.

His first destinations were the major centers of learning within Khurasan. Cities such as Merv and Herat offered opportunities to meet scholars who preserved chains of narration that differed from those in Naysabur. These journeys not only expanded his knowledge but also trained him in the hardships of travel. Long rides across arid lands, uncertain lodgings, and the physical demands of constant movement tested the determination of any student. Yet for Muslim, the purpose outweighed the discomfort. Each new teacher meant access to reports closer to the Prophet's era, each journey a step toward safeguarding the Sunnah.

From Khurasan, his travels extended farther westward. He journeyed to Iraq, the heart of the Abbasid Caliphate and a region dense with traditionists. Cities like Basra and Kufa had long been renowned for their scholars, many of whom had direct links to the companions of the Prophet through only a few generations. In these cities, Muslim encountered vast gatherings of students, where hundreds would sit to hear narrations recited. The scale of scholarship impressed him, but what mattered more was the chance to listen, compare, and verify.

It was in Iraq that Muslim encountered teachers whose reputations spanned the Islamic world. Among them were **Ishaq ibn Rahawayh**, **Ahmad ibn Hanbal**, and other towering figures of hadith scholarship. Sitting before these men, he absorbed lessons not only in transmission but also in discipline, patience, and piety. Each encounter strengthened his conviction that the pursuit of authentic knowledge was a lifelong commitment, not a temporary stage of study.

His journeys did not stop with Iraq. Like many of his contemporaries, Muslim travelled to the Hijaz, where the cities of Makkah and Madinah preserved unique chains of narration. Pilgrimage offered both a spiritual purpose and an academic one, for scholars from across the Muslim world gathered there during the seasons of Hajj. In those circles, Muslim had access to narrations transmitted by scholars who maintained the traditions of the companions who had lived and taught in the sacred cities.

Every journey left a mark on him. The hardships of travel tested his resolve, while the diversity of teachers broadened his perspective. He learned to compare reports from different regions, noting how the same narration might vary slightly depending on its transmitters. He also witnessed the seriousness with which senior scholars examined narrations, sometimes rejecting a report despite its popularity if a weakness was found in its chain. Such lessons deepened his own caution and sharpened his critical eye.

Through these travels, Muslim's reputation began to grow. Students and scholars alike recognized his sincerity, precision, and respect for the discipline of hadith. Though still young, he was no longer seen as merely a student from Naysabur but as a rising traditionist whose commitment matched that of the established masters. His journeys had opened the doors of the wider scholarly world to him, and each step along the road added to the foundation of the great work he would one day compile.

Chapter 7: Encounters with Renowned Scholars

As Muslim ibn al-Hajjaj advanced through his journeys, his encounters with renowned scholars left a lasting imprint on his scholarship. Each meeting offered him not only narrations to record but also lessons in methodology, discipline, and integrity. These figures represented the highest standards of hadith transmission, and their influence would shape his approach for the rest of his life.

Among the earliest of these encounters was his study with **Ishaq ibn Rahawayh**, one of the leading authorities of Khurasan. Known for his precision in hadith and strength in jurisprudence, Ishaq commanded respect among students and teachers alike. Muslim attended his lessons and absorbed his method of carefully weighing narrations before accepting them. Ishaq emphasized that hadith were not to be collected indiscriminately but filtered through rigorous standards. This caution resonated deeply with Muslim, strengthening the carefulness that already marked his character.

In Iraq, Muslim met **Ahmad ibn Hanbal**, the great scholar of Baghdad whose name would become associated with one of the four schools of Islamic jurisprudence. Ahmad's reputation rested not only on his vast knowledge of hadith but also on his steadfastness in times of trial. Muslim had the opportunity to hear narrations from him and to observe his deep humility before the words of the Prophet. The memory of Ahmad's patience during persecution under the Mihna, when he refused to compromise on the doctrine of the Qur'an, added another dimension to Muslim's understanding of what it meant to be a scholar: not only a transmitter of knowledge but a guardian of truth under pressure.

Equally influential was his connection with **Muhammad ibn Yahya al-Dhuhli**, a prominent traditionist of Naysabur who remained an anchor for students in the region. Al-Dhuhli introduced Muslim to further narrations and demonstrated how local scholarly networks could link into the broader world of transmission. His gatherings exposed Muslim to large assemblies where hundreds gathered to hear hadith recited, teaching him the importance of accuracy in both speaking and recording narrations before such audiences.

Perhaps most significant was his association with **Muhammad ibn Isma'il al-Bukhari**. Although both men would later compile works that stood as the most authentic collections of hadith, at this stage they were teacher and student. Muslim attended Bukhari's gatherings and absorbed his meticulous methods of authentication. Bukhari's insistence on the highest standards of continuity in chains of transmission and his attention to the reliability of each narrator set an example that Muslim studied closely. Though their methodologies would eventually diverge in certain respects, the respect Muslim carried for Bukhari's scholarship remained constant.

Beyond these figures, Muslim benefited from the knowledge of numerous other teachers across Khurasan, Iraq, the Hijaz, and Egypt. Each scholar added a thread to the fabric of his education. Some provided him with narrations transmitted through rare chains, while others impressed upon him the ethical dimension of scholarship—honesty in reporting, humility in teaching, and patience in correction. With every encounter, he broadened his horizons, refining not only his collection of hadith but also his character as a traditionist.

Through these relationships, Muslim was exposed to the diversity of scholarly thought within the Islamic world. He observed differences in the ways teachers approached questions of reliability, and he learned to respect the variety of perspectives that existed among sincere scholars. This exposure nurtured in him a balanced outlook: firm in his principles, yet aware of the nuances that came with transmitting knowledge across regions and generations.

Chapter 8: The Influence of Imam Ahmad ibn Hanbal

When Muslim ibn al-Hajjaj travelled to Baghdad, one of the towering figures of the scholarly world was Ahmad ibn Hanbal. Already known across the Islamic lands for his mastery of hadith and his steadfastness in faith, Imam Ahmad represented the embodiment of a scholar who combined knowledge, humility, and courage. For Muslim, the opportunity to sit in his gatherings and listen to his narrations was not only a privilege but also a formative stage in his development as a traditionist.

Ahmad ibn Hanbal's reputation rested above all on his devotion to hadith. His vast memorization, spanning hundreds of thousands of narrations, was matched by his careful standards of verification. Students who came to him found a teacher who refused to compromise on precision. Muslim absorbed this lesson keenly. In Ahmad's company, he witnessed how a scholar weighed the reliability of narrators, how he distinguished subtle differences between reports, and how he rejected narrations if even the smallest doubt arose about their authenticity.

Yet it was not Ahmad's knowledge alone that left an impression. His life had become a symbol of perseverance. During the Mihna—the inquisition imposed by the Abbasid rulers to enforce the belief that the Qur'an was created—Ahmad was imprisoned and beaten for refusing to adopt the official position. He endured suffering with patience, never abandoning his stance that the Qur'an was the uncreated word of God. For young students like Muslim, this story was not an abstract tale but a living example of the price a scholar might pay for holding to the truth. Ahmad's firmness demonstrated that scholarship carried responsibilities beyond the classroom; it demanded courage when faith was tested.

Muslim's time with Ahmad also showed him the humility of true scholarship. Despite his towering status, Ahmad lived simply, avoiding luxury and shunning political power. He taught his students that knowledge was not a means to fame or wealth but a trust to be preserved. Muslim, who was already inclined toward modesty, found in Ahmad a model of restraint and integrity. The simplicity of Ahmad's life reinforced the idea that scholarship required not only intellectual effort but also sincerity of intention.

In Ahmad's gatherings, Muslim also observed the interaction between a teacher and a wide circle of students. Scholars from across the Islamic world came to Baghdad to hear hadith from Ahmad, and the sessions often included students of varying backgrounds and abilities. Ahmad's patience with his listeners, his willingness to repeat narrations, and his emphasis on accuracy above speed taught Muslim how knowledge should be conveyed responsibly. These lessons would later influence his own role as a teacher in Naysabur.

While Muslim studied with many great scholars, the encounter with Ahmad ibn Hanbal gave his education a moral depth that complemented his technical training. From Ahmad, he inherited not only narrations but also the principles of steadfastness, humility, and sacrifice for the sake of truth. These qualities would stay with him long after he left Baghdad, becoming part of the foundation upon which his own scholarship would rest.

Chapter 9: The Role of Imam al-Bukhari

Among the many scholars Muslim ibn al-Hajjaj encountered in his travels, none had as profound an impact on his intellectual path as **Muhammad ibn Isma'il al-Bukhari**. By the time Muslim studied under him, al-Bukhari had already established himself as one of the foremost authorities in the science of hadith. His reputation for precision and integrity was unmatched, and his presence in Naysabur and other centers of learning attracted students from across the Islamic world.

Muslim was deeply drawn to al-Bukhari's methodology. Al-Bukhari's standards for accepting narrations were considered the most rigorous of his time. He demanded not only that the chain of transmission be unbroken but also that there be clear evidence of personal meeting between transmitters. This level of scrutiny, while controversial to some, set a new benchmark for authenticity. Muslim studied these methods carefully, observing how al-Bukhari sifted through vast numbers of narrations, discarding any that fell short of his criteria.

Their relationship was one of respect and devotion. Muslim attended al-Bukhari's gatherings with consistency, listening attentively and recording narrations. Accounts describe how Muslim openly expressed admiration for al-Bukhari, sometimes even declaring his loyalty in public. He defended his teacher against critics, recognizing the depth of scholarship and sincerity that characterized al-Bukhari's work. This loyalty was not blind, but rooted in genuine appreciation of al-Bukhari's contributions to the preservation of the Prophet's sayings.

At the same time, Muslim did not simply imitate al-Bukhari. While he adopted many of his teacher's principles, he also developed his own approach to compilation and authentication. For instance, where al-Bukhari demanded proof of direct meeting between narrators, Muslim was satisfied with strong evidence of possible encounter, provided the chain remained trustworthy. This difference reflected not a lack of respect but the independence of a scholar who combined admiration for his teacher with his own scholarly judgment.

The gatherings of al-Bukhari also exposed Muslim to the intensity of scholarly debates. Al-Bukhari faced opposition from some quarters, including disagreements with certain scholars of Naysabur. Muslim observed firsthand the tensions that could arise when high standards of hadith criticism challenged established practices. Rather than discouraging him, these disputes reinforced Muslim's conviction that the path of hadith scholarship required both courage and patience. He learned from al-Bukhari not only the technical methods of authentication but also the resilience needed to withstand criticism.

For Muslim, al-Bukhari embodied the unity of knowledge and character. His teacher's humility, his refusal to be swayed by worldly power, and his relentless devotion to accuracy provided a model of what a true scholar should be. These qualities left a deep mark on Muslim's own life, influencing not only the compilation of his work but also the way he carried himself as a scholar of integrity.

Through this relationship, Muslim gained more than narrations. He absorbed a vision of scholarship that placed truth above compromise, accuracy above convenience, and sincerity above recognition. His association with al-Bukhari was a turning point, one that would guide the direction of his own magnum opus and define his place among the great traditionists of Islam.

Chapter 10: Mastering the Sciences of Hadith

By the time Muslim ibn al-Hajjaj had returned to Naysabur after his extensive travels, he had accumulated not only vast collections of narrations but also a deep understanding of the principles governing their authenticity. His years of study under figures like Ahmad ibn Hanbal and al-Bukhari, combined with his personal rigor, allowed him to master the sciences of hadith in a way few of his contemporaries could claim.

The sciences of hadith required both memorization and critical analysis. Muslim had perfected the memorization of thousands of narrations, a skill essential for any scholar of the time. Yet memorization alone was insufficient. He had also developed the ability to scrutinize isnads—the chains of transmission—with exceptional care, noting the reliability, integrity, and temporal alignment of each transmitter. A single weak link could render a narration suspect, and Muslim's training had made him highly sensitive to such details.

He also mastered the classification of hadith. Muslim learned to distinguish between sahih (authentic), hasan (good), da'if (weak), and maudu' (fabricated) narrations. This categorization was not mechanical; it required nuanced judgment, contextual understanding, and a deep knowledge of each transmitter's biography. Muslim studied the lives of narrators meticulously, recording their habits, moral character, and reliability. This biographical scrutiny became one of his defining traits as a traditionist.

In addition to chains of transmission, Muslim was attentive to the text (matn) of narrations. He learned that inconsistencies or contradictions in content could indicate fabrication, especially if a narration conflicted with established teachings or other reliable reports. This dual approach—examining both chain and text—allowed him to filter reports with precision, reducing the risk of error in his own compilation.

Another aspect of mastery was his ability to organize narrations thematically. Muslim observed how his teachers, particularly al-Bukhari, arranged narrations by topic, which facilitated the use of hadith in legal rulings and ethical guidance. He began developing his own system, one that balanced accessibility with scholarly rigor. This organizational skill would later become a hallmark of his collection, distinguishing it from other works while maintaining its authority.

Muslim also understood the importance of corroboration. He compared narrations from different sources, cross-checking chains and texts to ensure accuracy. When discrepancies arose, he did not ignore them but investigated the circumstances of each report. This methodical approach demonstrated his commitment not only to collecting hadith but also to preserving the integrity of the Prophet's teachings for generations to come.

By mastering these sciences, Muslim had become a scholar capable of evaluating narrations independently while respecting the guidance of his teachers. His knowledge was both broad and deep, spanning regional traditions, differing methodologies, and the biographies of hundreds of narrators. The precision, patience, and critical insight he developed during this period laid the foundation for his lifelong work, ensuring that his contributions would endure as a model of scholarly excellence.

Chapter 11: Building a Reputation as a Scholar

By the time Muslim ibn al-Hajjaj returned to Naysabur fully trained in the sciences of hadith, his dedication and expertise began to attract attention from scholars and students alike. His reputation was not built overnight; it developed gradually through years of disciplined study, careful verification of narrations, and a steadfast commitment to honesty in transmission.

Word of his diligence spread quickly in scholarly circles. Students noticed his meticulous approach to chains of transmission, his ability to distinguish between authentic and weak reports, and his extensive memorization. Teachers recognized in him a rare combination of intelligence, patience, and humility. This growing acknowledgment gave Muslim access to larger gatherings, where he could engage with more advanced material and increasingly influential scholars.

Muslim's reputation was reinforced by his interactions with visiting scholars. Naysabur, a hub on the route of knowledge, regularly hosted teachers from Baghdad, Basra, Kufa, and beyond. These visitors observed Muslim's attention to detail and his willingness to question respectfully when clarification was needed. His methodical approach impressed even the most senior scholars, who began to recommend him as a trustworthy transmitter of hadith. This endorsement elevated his standing beyond the local community, connecting him with a network of scholars across the Islamic world.

The trust Muslim earned was also tied to his personal integrity. Unlike some students who sought recognition or material gain, he maintained a focus on accuracy and sincerity. Teachers and peers observed that he did not embellish narrations or accept reports without verification. His reputation as a scholar who valued truth over prestige became one of his defining traits. In a time when fabricated narrations circulated widely, this honesty distinguished him and made his word reliable in scholarly discourse.

His growing expertise allowed him to teach other students, further consolidating his standing. His lessons were structured, precise, and grounded in the rigorous methods he had learned from his teachers. Students who studied under him praised his clarity, his patience in explaining complex points, and his insistence on integrity in reporting. Through these teaching sessions, Muslim not only shared knowledge but also demonstrated the ethical and spiritual dimensions of scholarship, reinforcing his emerging reputation as a model scholar.

Beyond the classroom, Muslim's name circulated in written correspondence and through scholarly networks. Letters and reports from other cities acknowledged his reliability, and he began receiving requests to verify narrations or to provide guidance in matters of hadith. This recognition confirmed that his reputation was not confined to Naysabur but had reached a level of authority respected across regions.

By the end of this period, Muslim had established himself as a central figure in the field of hadith scholarship. His reputation rested on the combination of technical mastery, ethical integrity, and the ability to communicate knowledge effectively. These qualities laid the foundation for the monumental work he would undertake in the coming years, marking the beginning of his enduring influence in the Islamic scholarly tradition.

Chapter 12: The Vision for Sahih Muslim

As Muslim ibn al-Hajjaj matured in his scholarship, a vision began to take shape in his mind—an ambitious project that would define his legacy. Though he had collected and memorized countless narrations, he recognized a pressing need within the scholarly community: a comprehensive, rigorously authenticated compilation of hadith that could be relied upon without question. This need was intensified by the proliferation of weak and fabricated reports circulating in sermons, legal rulings, and religious discourse.

Muslim's insight was informed by his experience under the guidance of masters like al-Bukhari and Ahmad ibn Hanbal. From al-Bukhari, he learned the importance of strict criteria for authentication, including the requirement of continuous and reliable chains of transmission. From Ahmad ibn Hanbal, he absorbed the value of meticulous scrutiny, patience, and moral integrity. Combining these lessons, Muslim envisioned a work that would balance rigor with accessibility, providing scholars and students a reliable resource for years to come.

The vision was not merely technical; it carried a spiritual dimension. Muslim understood that preserving the Prophet's sayings accurately was a sacred responsibility. Each narration was more than a historical report—it was guidance for belief, practice, and conduct. His aim was to create a work that honoured this responsibility, one that reflected both the precision demanded by scholarship and the reverence due to the Prophet's message.

Early in the conception of his compilation, Muslim considered the practical challenges. The task required systematic organization, careful verification of thousands of narrations, and attention to the reliability of each transmitter. He needed to ensure that the final work could be used confidently by scholars of jurisprudence, theologians, and students alike. This foresight distinguished his approach from mere collections of narrations, which often lacked critical evaluation or structural clarity.

The vision also included a methodology for selection. Muslim resolved to include only narrations meeting the highest standards of authenticity. He intended to provide clear documentation of chains of transmission, ensuring that future scholars could trace each report back to its source. In addition, he contemplated organizing narrations according to topics, enabling practical application in legal and ethical matters. This dual focus—authenticity and usability—would later define the enduring value of his work.

Muslim's growing reputation as a reliable scholar gave him both the confidence and the support needed to pursue such an ambitious project. Teachers, peers, and students recognized the wisdom and integrity behind his plan, often encouraging him to proceed. At the same time, Muslim was aware of the enormity of the task; it required not only mastery of hadith but also years of dedication, travel, and consultation with other scholars.

This period marked the beginning of a transition from student and collector to author and compiler. The vision for what would become *Sahih Muslim* crystallized as both a scholarly and spiritual mission: to preserve the Prophet's teachings with precision, ensure their transmission without error, and provide an authoritative reference for generations to come.

Chapter 13: Principles of Selection

As Muslim ibn al-Hajjaj embarked on the monumental task of compiling his work, he established a set of principles that would guide his selection of narrations. These principles reflected both the rigorous standards he had learned from his teachers and his own understanding of what constituted reliability in hadith transmission.

The first and most fundamental principle was the continuity and integrity of the chain of transmission, or isnad. Muslim required that each narration have an unbroken chain connecting it to the Prophet Muhammad. He examined every transmitter in the chain, evaluating their moral character, accuracy in memorization, and reliability in reporting. Any link showing weakness or doubt was sufficient reason to exclude a narration. This attention to the integrity of the chain distinguished his compilation from collections that included weak or questionable reports.

A second principle involved the precision of the text, or matn. Muslim carefully scrutinized the wording of each narration, ensuring it did not conflict with established teachings of the Qur'an or other reliable hadith. He recognized that errors or inconsistencies in the text could undermine the credibility of a narration, even if the chain appeared sound. His sensitivity to textual accuracy reflected a deep understanding of the importance of clarity in religious guidance.

Corroboration was another key principle. Muslim often sought to verify narrations by comparing them with multiple chains of transmission. If a narration was reported through different reliable pathways, this strengthened its authenticity. Conversely, isolated reports or those that appeared in contradiction to other trusted narrations were subjected to careful scrutiny. This method allowed him to establish confidence in the reports he ultimately included.

Muslim also applied a principle of minimal repetition. While some narrations appeared multiple times with slight variations, he organized them to avoid redundancy while preserving necessary detail. Each report was placed in its proper context, often grouped according to legal, ethical, or theological topics. This organization enhanced the usability of the collection for students, scholars, and jurists.

Finally, intention and sincerity guided his selection. Muslim approached each narration not merely as a scholar recording history but as a custodian of divine guidance. He avoided inclusion of narrations that could be misused or that lacked sufficient reliability. His careful judgment reflected the ethical dimension of his work: preserving the teachings of the Prophet with integrity and ensuring that future generations would have a trustworthy source.

By adhering to these principles—integrity of the chain, precision of the text, corroboration, clarity in organization, and ethical responsibility—Muslim ibn al-Hajjaj set the framework for a compilation that would become one of the most respected and relied-upon collections of hadith in Islamic history.

Chapter 14: The Compilation Process

The process of compiling his magnum opus demanded meticulous planning and unwavering discipline from Muslim ibn al-Hajjaj. Having established the principles of selection, he set about the practical task of gathering, verifying, and arranging the thousands of narrations he had collected over decades of study and travel. The compilation process was as much an exercise in organization as it was in scholarship, requiring precision, patience, and memory.

Muslim began by reviewing the narrations he had amassed during his travels. These included reports memorized from teachers, written notes collected from gatherings, and chains obtained directly from scholars in cities such as Baghdad, Basra, Kufa, and the Hijaz. Each narration was cross-checked against other sources to verify its reliability. When discrepancies arose between reports from different teachers, he carefully examined the chains and biographies of transmitters to determine which account was most credible.

Organization played a crucial role in his work. Muslim arranged narrations thematically, grouping them according to topics relevant to law, ethics, prayer, and daily conduct. Within each section, he preserved the chains of transmission meticulously, providing readers with the ability to trace each narration back to its source. This careful structuring ensured that the work was both scholarly rigorous and practical for students and jurists who relied on it for guidance.

The verification process was exhaustive. Muslim did not accept a narration based solely on reputation or popularity. Each link in the isnad was scrutinized for integrity, reliability, and memory. Narrators who were known to exaggerate, forget, or misreport were excluded. Even narrations with minor weaknesses in transmission were set aside unless corroborated by other reliable chains. This painstaking attention to detail required years of sustained focus and an extraordinary memory.

During the compilation, Muslim also maintained correspondence with other scholars to clarify points of ambiguity or to confirm narrations from remote regions. Letters and reports allowed him to verify narrations from transmitters he could not meet in person. This collaborative aspect of his work ensured that the compilation was not confined to his own experience but represented a broader, authenticated scholarly consensus.

In addition to collection and verification, the act of arranging narrations demanded intellectual discernment. Muslim carefully decided the order in which narrations would appear, sometimes placing reports that emphasized legal rulings alongside similar reports that illustrated ethical principles. This deliberate sequencing enhanced the work's coherence, allowing readers to follow topics systematically and to understand the practical applications of the Prophet's teachings.

The physical act of writing was equally demanding. Muslim worked with painstaking care, ensuring accuracy in every transcription. Mistakes could compromise the authenticity of the work, so he reviewed and rewrote sections multiple times. Students and assistants occasionally aided in copying, but Muslim personally supervised the process to maintain the highest standards.

Through these laborious steps—gathering, verifying, organizing, consulting, and transcribing—Muslim ibn al-Hajjaj transformed decades of scholarship into a structured and authoritative collection. Each stage reflected his dedication to accuracy, his reverence for the Prophet's words, and his commitment to preserving knowledge for future generations.

Chapter 15: The Structure of Sahih Muslim

One of the distinguishing features of Muslim ibn al-Hajjaj's work lies in its meticulous structure. By the time he had completed the bulk of his compilation, he had established a system that allowed readers to navigate thousands of narrations with clarity, precision, and purpose. The organization of *Sahih Muslim* reflected both scholarly rigor and practical usability, setting it apart from earlier collections.

The compilation is arranged thematically, beginning with the fundamental aspects of faith and the pillars of Islam. Muslim placed narrations on belief, prayer, fasting, zakat, and pilgrimage at the forefront, establishing a foundation for readers to understand the core tenets of religious practice. Within these thematic divisions, narrations were sequenced carefully, often following a logical flow from general principles to specific applications. This order helped students grasp both the breadth and depth of Islamic teachings.

Each narration is presented with a complete chain of transmission, or isnad. Muslim carefully documented each narrator in the chain, sometimes providing brief notes on their reliability, memory, and moral character. This transparency allowed readers to verify the authenticity of the report independently, ensuring that the compilation remained a trustworthy reference for scholars and jurists. The presence of the isnad throughout the work reinforced the integrity of the collection and distinguished it from compilations that omitted such details.

Muslim also employed repetition strategically. While unnecessary duplication was avoided, narrations were sometimes included multiple times under different thematic headings to illustrate various legal or ethical points. This technique enabled readers to see how a single report could inform multiple areas of study without sacrificing accuracy. In this way, the structure served both scholarly analysis and practical application.

Another feature of the work is its balance between legal and ethical guidance. Muslim did not limit his selection to rulings or jurisprudential matters; he also included narrations that conveyed moral principles, etiquette, and guidance for everyday conduct. This dual focus reflected his understanding that hadith were a comprehensive source of instruction, encompassing belief, practice, and character.

Cross-referencing within the collection further enhanced its usability. Related narrations were often cited together, allowing readers to compare and contrast reports on similar topics. This organization encouraged critical engagement with the material, enabling scholars to draw nuanced conclusions based on multiple sources. The careful arrangement of narrations made *Sahih Muslim* not only a repository of knowledge but also a tool for reasoning and teaching.

Finally, the clarity of language and consistency in presentation contributed to the work's enduring value. Muslim avoided ambiguity in the text, maintaining a style that prioritized precision without sacrificing readability. Each section, narration, and chain of transmission was presented systematically, reflecting the careful thought and discipline invested in the compilation.

Through this carefully planned structure, Muslim ibn al-Hajjaj ensured that *Sahih Muslim* would be both authoritative and accessible, guiding generations of scholars, students, and jurists in the study and application of the Prophet's teachings.

Chapter 16: Challenges and Criticisms

Despite the monumental achievement of his compilation, Muslim ibn al-Hajjaj faced numerous challenges and criticisms during and after the creation of his work. The rigorous standards he applied in selecting narrations, while lauded by many, also provoked questions and debates among scholars of his time. These challenges shaped both the reception of his work and his approach to defending its integrity.

One of the primary challenges was the sheer scale of the task. Muslim travelled extensively to collect narrations from scholars across the Islamic world. Each journey involved physical hardship, from long desert crossings to uncertain accommodations, and demanded significant mental focus. Managing thousands of narrations, verifying the reliability of every transmitter, and cross-checking chains required extraordinary discipline and perseverance. Even minor lapses could compromise the credibility of the compilation, placing immense responsibility on him.

Criticism also arose from scholars who differed in methodology. Some questioned whether his standards of authentication were too strict, arguing that certain narrations excluded from his collection might still hold value. Others contended that his work relied heavily on chains that, while strong in his judgment, could be challenged by alternative chains known in other regions. Muslim faced these critiques not defensively but through meticulous explanation and adherence to the principles he had established, demonstrating that his selection process was both systematic and principled.

Another challenge stemmed from the diverse scholarly climate of the time. The Islamic world was not monolithic; regional traditions and varying interpretations of hadith science sometimes led to disagreement. Scholars in Baghdad, Basra, Kufa, and Naysabur each had their preferred narrators and chains of transmission. Muslim navigated these differences by documenting the biographies of transmitters thoroughly and providing detailed isnads, allowing readers to assess the authenticity of narrations independently. His careful documentation helped mitigate disputes and reinforced the credibility of his work.

Fabrication of narrations also presented an ongoing concern. In an era when weak or false reports circulated widely, even minor errors could lead to misguidance. Muslim dedicated significant effort to identifying such reports, excluding narrations from questionable transmitters, and cross-referencing multiple chains. This diligence sometimes drew criticism from those who favoured quantity over strict scrutiny, but Muslim's commitment to accuracy remained unwavering.

Finally, social and political pressures added to the difficulty of his work. As a scholar dependent on access to teachers, manuscripts, and audiences, he had to navigate complex social networks. Respect for local authorities and adherence to societal norms required careful judgment. Yet Muslim consistently prioritized scholarly integrity over convenience or popularity, ensuring that the compilation reflected truth rather than compromise.

Through these challenges—physical, methodological, and social—Muslim's work faced scrutiny and debate. Yet these very difficulties underscore the discipline, patience, and intellectual rigor required to produce a compilation that would become one of the most respected sources in Islamic scholarship.

Chapter 17: Completion of a Magnum Opus

After decades of rigorous travel, study, verification, and compilation, Muslim ibn al-Hajjaj reached the stage of completing his magnum opus, *Sahih Muslim*. The process was the culmination of a lifetime devoted to the meticulous collection and authentication of the Prophet's sayings, a task that required unparalleled dedication, patience, and intellectual discipline.

Completion did not occur suddenly; it was the result of careful revision and refinement. Muslim reviewed the thousands of narrations he had collected, double-checking chains of transmission and cross-referencing multiple sources. He ensured that each narration met his stringent criteria for authenticity, removing any report that failed to satisfy his meticulous standards. His careful editing reinforced the credibility of the work and distinguished it from other collections, many of which included weaker reports.

Organization played a critical role in the final stages. Muslim arranged narrations thematically, grouping them according to topics such as faith, prayer, transactions, ethics, and social conduct. Within each section, he ordered the narrations to provide logical progression, highlighting related reports and facilitating comparison between narrations with similar content. This methodical structure allowed scholars and students to navigate the work efficiently, making it both a reference and a teaching tool.

Muslim also ensured that his compilation reflected both breadth and depth. He included narrations widely transmitted as well as rare reports he obtained from specific teachers or distant regions. This combination gave the work comprehensive coverage of the Prophet's teachings, preserving not only the most common traditions but also those that might otherwise have been lost to time. His attention to diverse sources reinforced the scholarly reliability of the compilation.

The physical preparation of the manuscript demanded precision. Muslim supervised the transcription of narrations, reviewing each section personally to avoid errors. Scribes assisted in copying, but Muslim's oversight ensured the integrity of the text. Marginal notes and annotations were sometimes added to clarify chains of transmission or to distinguish narrations with multiple versions, demonstrating his commitment to accuracy and clarity.

Completion of *Sahih Muslim* marked the transformation of a life devoted to learning into a tangible, enduring contribution to Islamic scholarship. The work was not merely a compilation of narrations but a carefully structured, critically verified, and ethically guided reference. Its preparation reflected Muslim's mastery of hadith sciences, his methodological rigor, and his unwavering dedication to preserving the Prophet's teachings for generations to come.

Chapter 18: Teaching and Guiding Students

While Muslim ibn al-Hajjaj's reputation as a collector and verifier of hadith grew, he also dedicated significant effort to teaching and guiding students. His role as a mentor was inseparable from his work as a scholar; he recognized that the preservation and transmission of knowledge depended not only on written compilations but also on the cultivation of disciplined, ethical learners.

Muslim's teaching style reflected the methods he had observed in his own teachers. He emphasized careful listening, precise recording, and critical examination of narrations. Students were expected to memorize reports accurately and to understand the principles governing their authentication. Muslim insisted that a student's integrity, humility, and respect for the chain of transmission were as important as intellectual ability. Those who came to study under him were trained to approach hadith not merely as texts but as a sacred trust.

His sessions often involved detailed explanation of isnads and narrators' biographies. Muslim would provide context for each chain of transmission, noting potential weaknesses, discrepancies, or corroborating sources. This meticulous attention to detail allowed students to develop independent judgment while learning to rely on scholarly methodology. He frequently stressed that the student must verify and understand each narration, rather than accepting reports unquestioningly.

Beyond technical instruction, Muslim imparted lessons in character and ethics. He modeled patience, humility, and steadfastness in study, emphasizing that true scholarship required sincerity and moral responsibility. Students observed his disciplined habits, from his careful transcription of narrations to his unwavering attention during teaching sessions. This example reinforced the notion that knowledge and virtue were inseparable in the pursuit of Islamic scholarship.

Muslim's reputation drew students from far and wide. Many travelled long distances to sit under his guidance, seeking access to the knowledge he had acquired through years of travel and study. His gatherings became hubs of learning, where students could compare chains, discuss narrations, and learn to discern authenticity. The interaction among students and their teacher fostered a culture of collaboration, critical thinking, and respect for the rigor of hadith sciences.

In addition to in-person instruction, Muslim often provided guidance to students who were unable to study with him directly. Letters and written explanations clarified narrations and methodologies, extending his influence beyond Naysabur. Through this combination of personal mentorship and scholarly correspondence, he ensured that the next generation of traditionists would uphold the same standards of accuracy and integrity that had defined his own work.

Through his dedication to teaching, Muslim not only preserved the knowledge he had compiled but also created a community of scholars capable of continuing the rigorous study of hadith. His students carried forward his principles, ensuring that the methodologies, ethical standards, and intellectual rigor he cultivated remained central to Islamic scholarship for generations.

Chapter 19: Personal Character and Piety

Alongside his scholarly achievements, Muslim ibn al-Hajjaj was renowned for his personal character and devotion to piety. His life exemplified the integration of knowledge and virtue, demonstrating that mastery of hadith required not only intellectual discipline but also moral integrity and spiritual commitment.

Muslim was widely respected for his humility. Despite his growing reputation, he never sought fame or personal gain from his scholarship. He lived modestly, avoiding ostentation and worldly excess. Students and peers noted his consistent adherence to ethical conduct, both in public gatherings and in private interactions. This humility reinforced the credibility of his work, as those who studied under him observed that his teachings were motivated by sincerity rather than ambition.

Piety shaped every aspect of his life. Muslim maintained regular prayer, fasting, and other acts of worship, integrating them seamlessly with his scholarly pursuits. His devotion was evident in his meticulous attention to study, which he treated as both an intellectual and spiritual discipline. He approached the Prophet's sayings with reverence, understanding that transmitting hadith was an act of service to God and the community.

Truthfulness was a defining trait. Muslim adhered strictly to accuracy in reporting narrations, never allowing personal bias or external influence to affect his judgment. This commitment to honesty extended beyond scholarship into daily life, earning him the trust and admiration of peers, teachers, and students alike. His moral steadfastness became a model for aspiring scholars, emphasizing that character and knowledge must advance together.

Muslim also displayed patience and perseverance, qualities essential to enduring the hardships of travel, long hours of study, and the challenges of verification. His journeys to distant cities, often under difficult conditions, were undertaken with unwavering dedication. He approached every obstacle as part of his responsibility to preserve authentic teachings, demonstrating both resilience and steadfastness in the face of adversity.

Generosity of spirit further marked his personal character. Muslim was approachable to students, always willing to answer questions, clarify doubts, and guide learners with patience and kindness. He valued their progress and encouraged independent thinking within the framework of scholarly rigor, fostering a supportive environment for the pursuit of knowledge.

Through the combination of humility, devotion, truthfulness, patience, and generosity, Muslim ibn al-Hajjaj embodied the ideal of a scholar whose personal character reinforced the authority and credibility of his work. His life demonstrated that piety and scholarship were inseparable, and that the preservation of hadith demanded not only intellectual mastery but also ethical and spiritual excellence.

Chapter 20: Family and Private Life

Despite the immense demands of scholarship, Muslim ibn al-Hajjaj maintained a life grounded in family and private affairs. Though historical records focus primarily on his intellectual contributions, glimpses of his domestic life reveal a man who balanced rigorous study with the responsibilities and relationships of home.

Muslim valued family as a source of support and stability. Accounts indicate that he treated relatives with respect and kindness, fulfilling obligations to parents, siblings, and extended kin. His upbringing in Naysabur, a city known for both its scholarly atmosphere and its strong social networks, instilled in him the importance of familial ties alongside academic pursuits. He maintained these connections even during his travels, writing letters and arranging visits whenever possible to remain close to his family.

His private life was marked by simplicity, mirroring his public ethos of humility. Muslim avoided extravagance in dress, food, and living arrangements, choosing instead a modest lifestyle that allowed him to focus on study and spiritual practice. This simplicity extended to his household, where he balanced domestic responsibilities with the demands of teaching and compiling hadith.

While Muslim devoted much of his time to scholarship, he did not neglect the moral and spiritual education of his family. Sources suggest that he encouraged prayer, ethical behavior, and study of Islamic teachings within the household, emphasizing the integration of religious knowledge into everyday life. His example demonstrated that scholarship was not separate from domestic life but a framework through which faith, ethics, and responsibility could be cultivated in personal relationships.

Marriage and children, though less documented, appear to have been conducted in accordance with the social norms of his time. Muslim treated family obligations with seriousness, ensuring that his responsibilities as a husband or father—if he had children—did not interfere with his commitment to study, yet he also did not allow scholarship to overshadow moral and ethical duties at home. His private life thus reflected a disciplined balance between devotion to knowledge and devotion to family.

Even in moments of leisure or rest, Muslim maintained spiritual mindfulness. Anecdotes recount that he would often recite prayers, reflect on the Prophet's teachings, or engage in private study during intervals away from formal scholarly gatherings. This integration of devotion into daily life reinforced the coherence between his public scholarship and private conduct, presenting a holistic example of a life devoted to knowledge, faith, and ethical responsibility.

Through the interplay of family life, personal discipline, and scholarly rigor, Muslim ibn al-Hajjaj exemplified a model in which intellectual achievement and domestic virtue complemented one another. His private life offered insight into the personal qualities—humility, devotion, balance, and ethical integrity—that underpinned his enduring contributions to Islamic scholarship.

Chapter 21: Final Years

In the later years of his life, Muslim ibn al-Hajjaj continued to teach, guide students, and refine his work, while the intensity of his travels gradually lessened. These years marked a period of consolidation, reflection, and quiet scholarship, during which he focused on ensuring the enduring integrity of his compilation and the knowledge he had accumulated over decades.

By this stage, Muslim had established a settled routine in Naysabur. His days were divided between study, teaching, and worship. Students still gathered to hear him recite narrations and explain the principles of hadith verification, while he devoted hours to revisiting his manuscripts, correcting minor errors, and ensuring that the chains of transmission remained accurate. His meticulous attention to detail persisted, reflecting the same standards that had guided him throughout his scholarly career.

Though he travelled less frequently, Muslim maintained correspondence with scholars in other cities, exchanging letters to clarify narrations, confirm chains of transmission, and discuss methodological issues. This practice allowed him to remain connected to the broader scholarly world while preserving his health and dedicating more time to teaching. The networks he had cultivated over decades ensured that his influence continued to extend far beyond Naysabur.

His personal life during these years remained disciplined and spiritually oriented. Muslim observed his daily prayers with devotion, fasted regularly, and engaged in reflection on the teachings of the Prophet. The simplicity of his lifestyle, already evident in his earlier years, continued uninterrupted, reinforcing the alignment between his scholarly rigor and personal piety. Students and visitors noted his humility, approachability, and patience, qualities that made him not only a respected scholar but also a beloved teacher and mentor.

Health challenges gradually emerged, as is natural with age, but Muslim's commitment to study did not waver. He continued to receive students, answer questions, and oversee the transcription of his works, demonstrating a remarkable dedication to the preservation of knowledge. His daily routines emphasized continuity, ensuring that the standards he had established in his life and scholarship were transmitted faithfully to the next generation.

During this period, Muslim also reflected on the broader significance of his work. He remained aware of the responsibility inherent in preserving the sayings of the Prophet, recognizing that his compilation would serve as a reference for scholars, jurists, and students for centuries to come. This sense of purpose lent both discipline and calm to his final years, as he balanced the demands of scholarship with the contemplative awareness of his life's spiritual mission.

Through steadfast dedication to teaching, meticulous care in refining his work, and continued devotion to spiritual practice, the final years of Muslim ibn al-Hajjaj were marked by a quiet but profound influence, consolidating a legacy built over decades of scholarship, travel, and ethical commitment.

Chapter 22: Passing of Imam Muslim

The life of Muslim ibn al-Hajjaj, after decades of tireless scholarship and pious devotion, came to its natural close in the city of Naysabur. His passing marked the end of an era for students and scholars who had witnessed firsthand the dedication, precision, and integrity that defined his work.

Accounts describe his final days as reflective and tranquil. Though his health had gradually declined, he remained conscious of his responsibilities as a scholar. He continued to teach and guide students until he was no longer able, maintaining his routines of worship and study. Friends and pupils observed him in his last moments demonstrating the same humility and piety that had characterized his entire life.

The news of his passing spread quickly through Naysabur and neighbouring regions. Scholars who had studied under him, as well as those who knew him by reputation, gathered to pay their respects. His students mourned the loss of a teacher whose influence extended far beyond the memorization of hadith; they had also inherited his commitment to ethical scholarship, patience, and moral integrity.

Muslim was interred in Naysabur, the city where his scholarly journey had begun and where he had spent much of his life teaching and refining his work. Reports suggest that his burial was attended by both family and scholars from the region, reflecting the broad esteem in which he was held. Tributes emphasized his rigorous methodology, his moral character, and his role in preserving the sayings of the Prophet with unparalleled accuracy.

The passing of Imam Muslim did not diminish the influence of his work. *Sahih Muslim* had already begun to circulate widely among scholars, students, and jurists. His meticulous compilation and the principles he had established ensured that his contributions would endure beyond his lifetime. In this way, his death was both a moment of personal loss for those who knew him and a milestone in the ongoing preservation of Islamic knowledge.

Even after his passing, Muslim ibn al-Hajjaj's life continued to serve as a model for scholars. His integrity, diligence, and devotion to both faith and learning became an enduring reference for students of hadith, setting a standard for those who sought to follow in his footsteps.

Chapter 23: Impact of Sahih Muslim

The compilation of *Sahih Muslim* left an immediate and lasting impact on the Islamic scholarly world. Unlike many collections of hadith that circulated with varying degrees of authenticity, Muslim ibn al-Hajjaj's work quickly became recognized as a rigorous, reliable reference for scholars, jurists, and students alike. Its meticulous methodology and adherence to the principles of verification set a new standard in hadith scholarship.

In the years following its completion, scholars praised the precision of the isnads and the careful arrangement of narrations. *Sahih Muslim* became a primary reference alongside *Sahih al-Bukhari*, providing scholars with confidence in its authenticity. The clarity and organization of the work made it particularly useful for legal scholars, who relied on it to support jurisprudential rulings, and for theologians, who drew on it for guidance in matters of belief and ethical practice.

The influence of *Sahih Muslim* extended across geographic and cultural boundaries. Scholars in Baghdad, Damascus, Egypt, and beyond incorporated the work into their teaching and research. Its reliability encouraged widespread citation and discussion, fostering a scholarly culture in which verification, critical analysis, and careful documentation became essential practices. Muslim's method of corroborating narrations through multiple chains influenced subsequent generations of hadith scholars and ensured a higher standard of precision in later compilations.

The work also shaped the approach of students learning the science of hadith. Teachers consistently directed students to study *Sahih Muslim* for examples of authentic narration, detailed chains of transmission, and well-organized thematic content. Its clarity enabled learners to understand both the methodology and the content of hadith scholarship, cultivating a generation of scholars trained in critical evaluation and careful reporting.

Beyond the academic sphere, *Sahih Muslim* contributed to religious life in broader society. Its narrations guided everyday practice, informed sermons, and served as a basis for personal piety. The accessibility of the thematic arrangement allowed individuals and communities to implement the teachings of the Prophet with confidence in their authenticity. In this way, the work bridged the gap between scholarly rigor and practical application.

Over time, *Sahih Muslim* became one of the most cited and respected collections in Sunni Islam. Its influence can be traced in legal rulings, theological writings, and educational curricula for centuries. By setting a high standard of verification and organization, Muslim ibn al-Hajjaj transformed the compilation of hadith into a disciplined, replicable, and authoritative enterprise, securing his place as one of the most influential scholars in Islamic history.

Chapter 24: Comparison with Other Hadith Works

Muslim ibn al-Hajjaj's *Sahih Muslim* is often examined in comparison with other major hadith collections, most notably *Sahih al-Bukhari*. While both works are esteemed for their authenticity, their methodologies, structure, and focus reveal subtle yet significant distinctions that reflect the individual approaches of their compilers.

One of the most notable differences lies in methodology. Imam al-Bukhari required direct evidence that each transmitter in a chain had met the one before him, placing extreme emphasis on the personal encounter. Muslim, while equally rigorous, allowed narrations from reliable transmitters whose meeting was not definitively documented, provided there was strong evidence of continuity. This distinction gave *Sahih Muslim* a slightly broader base of authentic narrations while maintaining the highest standards of verification.

The organizational structure also distinguishes the two works. *Sahih al-Bukhari* often includes extensive introductory remarks for each section, explaining legal implications, theological principles, or methodological considerations. Muslim opted for a more streamlined presentation, arranging narrations thematically with minimal commentary. This approach made *Sahih Muslim* highly accessible for students seeking clarity and direct reference, while still preserving rigorous chains of transmission.

Coverage and selection criteria present further contrasts. Both compilers exercised careful judgment in excluding weak or fabricated narrations, but Muslim occasionally included narrations that illustrated ethical or spiritual principles, even if they were less central to legal rulings. Bukhari's focus tended to emphasize the most rigorously verified reports that directly informed legal and doctrinal matters. This difference reflects Muslim's intention to balance jurisprudential relevance with comprehensive moral guidance.

The use of repetition and cross-referencing also varies. Muslim strategically repeated narrations under different thematic sections to facilitate comparative study, whereas Bukhari often prioritized a single, well-documented placement. This organizational choice in *Sahih Muslim* enhanced its usability for scholars seeking to examine related reports on a variety of topics without compromising authenticity.

Despite these differences, both works share a commitment to meticulous verification, moral integrity, and the preservation of prophetic teachings. Together, they form complementary pillars of Sunni hadith scholarship, each reflecting the unique vision and methodology of its compiler. Where Bukhari's work emphasizes precision through strict criteria of meeting narrators, Muslim's compilation demonstrates a disciplined flexibility that allows a slightly broader but still authentic range of narrations.

The comparison also underscores the influence of teacher-student relationships. Muslim studied under Bukhari and other prominent scholars, absorbing methods and principles that he adapted to his own approach. This dynamic illustrates how early hadith scholarship evolved through rigorous observation, critical thinking, and respectful adaptation of proven methodologies.

In sum, examining *Sahih Muslim* alongside other collections highlights both the shared commitment to authenticity and the unique contributions of each compiler. Muslim's work stands out for its thematic clarity, careful balance between verification and accessibility, and thoughtful inclusion of narrations that guide both ethical conduct and legal understanding.

Chapter 25: Transmission Through the Ages

The enduring influence of *Sahih Muslim* depends not only on its compilation but also on the meticulous preservation and transmission carried out by generations of scholars and students. From the moment it was completed, the work became a cornerstone of Islamic learning, copied, taught, and disseminated with great care across the Islamic world.

Initially, transmission relied on oral recitation and direct study under those who had access to the original compilation. Students travelled long distances to sit with teachers who had memorized the narrations, ensuring that the content and chains of transmission were accurately preserved. This oral method emphasized memorization, careful recitation, and verification, reflecting the same principles Muslim had applied in assembling his work.

Manuscript copying further extended the reach of *Sahih Muslim.* Early scribes reproduced the text with careful attention to accuracy, often including marginal notes to clarify chains of transmission or variant readings. These copies were circulated to major centers of learning such as Baghdad, Damascus, Cairo, and later to North Africa and Andalusia. Each manuscript became a resource for scholars who relied on it for teaching, research, and the verification of narrations.

In addition to direct study and manuscript copying, students and scholars compiled commentaries and explanations to accompany *Sahih Muslim.* These works elucidated complex chains of narrators, clarified obscure points, and provided guidance for applying narrations to legal and ethical matters. This body of commentary reinforced the accuracy of transmission while expanding the accessibility of Muslim's work for successive generations.

Educational institutions played a vital role in transmission. Madrasas and informal study circles incorporated *Sahih Muslim* into their curricula, teaching students the principles of verification and the structure of thematic arrangement. Scholars emphasized the importance of memorizing both the narrations and their chains, ensuring that the integrity of the work remained intact even as it spread geographically and across generations.

Over the centuries, *Sahih Muslim* continued to influence scholars far beyond its place of origin. Its transmission was not merely a mechanical copying of text; it involved active engagement, teaching, and critical study. Students of different regions contributed to its preservation, sometimes reconciling variant readings and validating narrators to maintain consistency with Muslim's original methodology.

The cumulative effect of these efforts ensured that *Sahih Muslim* retained its authority and accessibility. Through memorization, manuscript reproduction, teaching, and commentary, the compilation became a living tradition, continually renewed by scholars who honoured the principles of accuracy, integrity, and reverence established by its compiler.

Chapter 26: Imam Muslim's Place in History

Imam Muslim ibn al-Hajjaj occupies a central and enduring place in the history of Islamic scholarship. His contributions extend far beyond the compilation of *Sahih Muslim*; they shaped the methodology, standards, and ethos of hadith study for generations of scholars.

His position is often considered alongside other luminaries of the field, particularly Imam al-Bukhari. While both achieved unparalleled rigor in collecting and verifying hadith, Muslim's work is distinguished by its thematic clarity, methodological transparency, and balance between strict authentication and accessibility. Scholars have consistently recognized him as one of the foremost traditionists, whose judgment and discernment set benchmarks for reliability and precision.

Imam Muslim's influence is evident in the generations of scholars who followed him. Students who studied under him carried forward his principles of verification, ethical responsibility, and careful documentation, ensuring the continuity of rigorous hadith scholarship. His methods were adapted and refined by later scholars, yet the foundation he established remained central to the discipline.

Beyond academic circles, his work shaped Islamic law, ethics, and practice. *Sahih Muslim* provided jurists with reliable reports that informed legal rulings, while its narrations guided moral conduct, personal devotion, and social interaction. The work became an indispensable reference for both scholars and students, creating a bridge between rigorous scholarship and the lived experience of the Muslim community.

Imam Muslim's place in history is also reinforced by the enduring reverence for his personal character. Accounts of his humility, piety, integrity, and devotion to knowledge serve as a model for both scholars and laypeople. His life demonstrates that intellectual achievement in

Islam is inseparable from ethical conduct, spiritual devotion, and the responsible transmission of knowledge.

Historically, his influence has been international in scope. From the early centers of learning in Khorasan and Baghdad to regions as far as North Africa and Andalusia, scholars relied on his compilation as a primary source of hadith. Institutions of learning incorporated *Sahih Muslim* into their curricula, ensuring that his contributions remained central to Islamic education across diverse cultural and geographic contexts.

In evaluating the history of Islamic scholarship, Imam Muslim stands as a figure whose work represents both a pinnacle of intellectual rigor and a model of ethical and spiritual discipline. His contributions endure not only in the text of *Sahih Muslim* but also in the standards, principles, and values he imparted to subsequent generations, securing his legacy as one of the most influential scholars in the history of Islam.

Chapter 27: Lessons from Imam Muslim's Life

The life of Imam Muslim ibn al-Hajjaj offers a rich source of guidance for scholars, students, and anyone seeking to understand the principles of learning, ethics, and devotion. Across the span of his experiences, several key lessons emerge that illuminate the qualities essential for both intellectual and spiritual growth.

First and foremost, his dedication to scholarship demonstrates the value of perseverance. From his earliest days in Naysabur, through decades of travel to distant cities, and into his later years refining *Sahih Muslim*, Muslim exemplified unwavering commitment. He teaches that mastery of knowledge requires continuous effort, discipline, and resilience, even in the face of physical hardship or intellectual challenge.

Equally important is his insistence on accuracy and integrity. Muslim's meticulous attention to the chains of transmission and the content of narrations underscores the importance of precision and honesty in scholarship. His example shows that knowledge gains credibility only when it is pursued with ethical rigor, emphasizing that intellectual achievement must be rooted in moral responsibility.

Humility and piety were central to his life. Despite his growing reputation and influence, Muslim remained humble, modest, and deeply devoted to worship. He models the integration of learning with spiritual practice, teaching that knowledge and faith reinforce one another rather than existing in isolation. His life demonstrates that true scholarship is inseparable from ethical conduct and personal devotion.

Muslim also illustrates the importance of mentorship and teaching. By guiding students with patience, clarity, and moral example, he ensured that the principles and methodologies he developed would endure beyond his lifetime. His commitment to education underscores the broader responsibility of scholars to cultivate the next generation, creating a chain of knowledge and integrity that mirrors the isnad he so carefully preserved in hadith.

Adaptability and critical thinking are further lessons from his work. Muslim balanced rigorous standards with practical judgment, navigating differing regional traditions, varied narrators, and complex chains of transmission. His life shows that adherence to principle does not preclude flexibility in application and that thoughtful discernment is essential in the pursuit of truth.

Finally, his integration of public and private life offers guidance in achieving balance. Muslim maintained ethical and spiritual discipline at home, with family, and in private reflection, as well as in his public scholarly activities. He exemplifies how intellectual rigor, moral responsibility, and personal piety can coexist in a harmonious, productive life.

Through perseverance, integrity, humility, mentorship, critical thinking, and balance, the life of Imam Muslim ibn al-Hajjaj provides enduring lessons. His example continues to inspire scholars and believers alike, offering a model of how knowledge, ethics, and devotion can intersect to leave a lasting impact on both individual lives and the broader community.

www.ingramcontent.com/pod-product-compliance
Lightning Source LLC
LaVergne TN
LVHW090432210926
848480LV00002B/793
* 9 7 9 8 2 3 2 2 4 3 2 9 6 *